a home afloat

living aboard vessels of all shapes and sizes

Gary Cookson

ADLARD COLES NAUTICAL

LONDON

Published by
Adlard Coles Nautical
an imprint of A & C Black
Publishers Ltd
38 Soho Square
London W1D 3HB
www.adlardcoles.com

First published in Australia in
2005 by 20/21 Publications.

Second edition published by
Adlard Coles Nautical 2008.

ISBN 978-07136-8877-1

A CIP catalogue record for
this book is available from the
British Library.

This book is produced using
paper that is made from wood
grown in managed, sustainable
forests. It is natural, renewable
and recyclable. The logging and
manufacturing processes conform
to the environmental regulations
of the country of origin.

Typeset in Janson 9pt
Printed and bound by Star
Standard Industries (Pte) Ltd,
Singapore.

Note: while all reasonable
care has been taken in the
publication of this book, the
publisher takes no responsibility
for the use of the methods or
products described in the book.

Photographs and images are
used with permission. See
individual credits.
Design: 20/21 Design Services.
www.twentytwentyone.net

If you have an interesting ship
or floating home that you would
like to see featured in a future
edition please contact us at
info@twentytwentyone.net

Contents

Introduction

On rivers, canals, seas and lakes all over the world you'll find a diverse bunch of people who have chosen to trade a traditional home of bricks and mortar for the freedom of life on the water. In floating craft, large or small, with all the comforts of home, these happy liveaboards prove that home is where the heart is.

Living afloat holds many attractions – for some it's the love of water and being close to nature. For others it's a lifestyle choice – the ability to build a home that can be moved from place to place when you get tired of your surroundings. A floating home can offer a flexible way of life that you can't achieve in a conventional house or apartment. Imagine waking up to the sound of ducks quacking next to your bedroom window, or looking outside to a different view every day and you start to get the idea.

Idyllic as it sounds, life afloat is not without its challenges. Moorings, especially in big cities, can be very hard to find and are often expensive. Boats can have many of the same upkeep problems as a house with the added risk of sinking. A boat or ship doesn't tend to appreciate in value at the same rate as a house and will require more maintenance of a specialised nature. Larger ships need to come out of the water at least every five years for a survey to satisfy an insurer, which can be a very disruptive process if it is your only home.

For all the disadvantages however, there are many people who would never go back to a conventional house and are happily floating around the waterways of the world taking their home with them wherever they go.

This book lets you take a peek through the portholes of some amazing floating homes – from boats that are permanently moored, to ones that are permanently travelling, or somewhere in between. And just like their skippers and crew they come in all shapes and sizes with budgets large and small.

If you've ever wandered along a foreshore, riverbank or canal towpath and wondered what those unusual floating homes look like inside, then turn the page and find out.

RIGHT: *David Jay's home* Trimilia *is an ex-lifeboat converted into a sailing yacht. He lives aboard and runs his business from one of the cabins.*
See page 120.

Vessel Types

There are many different types of boats and ships suitable for living afloat. It is impossible to give a definitive guide but these are some of the most common types.

page 13   page 67   page 91

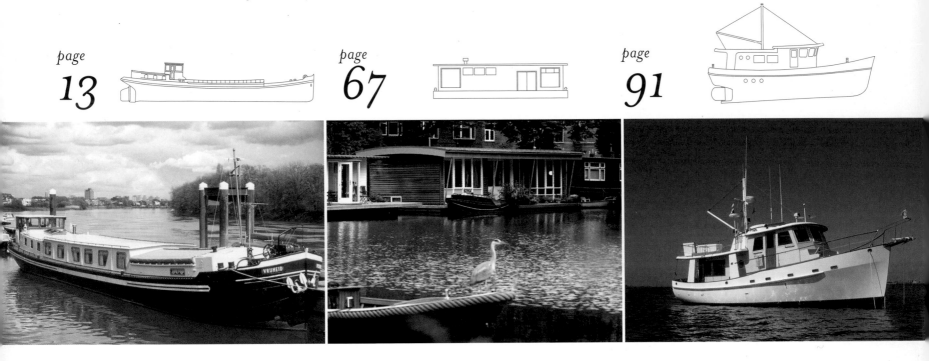

Barges

Ships that come under the general title of barge are usually ex-commercial carrying vessels that were used to transport cargo on the canals and rivers of Europe. There are also modern replica barges being built.

Size varies enormously but the vessels of around 80ft (25m) or less are the most popular. In their trading life, like British narrowboats, an entire family would have lived aboard in a small cabin at the rear of the boat, the rest of the ship being used for cargo. With a converted barge it is this old cargo area that becomes accommodation.

Houseboats

Houseboats can be divided into two basic types.

The first uses the hull of a ship that has had most of its machinery removed. Living accommodation is created within this space and often a new superstructure is built on top.

The second type of houseboat is a purpose-built floating structure designed solely for housing purposes. Essentially it is a wood- or steel-framed house built on a floating pontoon. The pontoon is usually a square or rectangular shape constructed of steel or concrete. The concrete variety is almost maintenance-free, unlike steel-hulled houseboats which have to be taken out of the water regularly for inspection and treatment against rust.

Both types of houseboat are usually permanently moored and can be connected to mains sewerage and services.

Motor Cruisers and Motor Yachts

Motor cruisers are engine-powered boats of around 25ft (7.5m) to 46ft (14m). Larger vessels of 50ft (15m) and above tend to be called motor yachts. Designs vary significantly according to their purpose, but for their given length they can offer a lot of living accommodation.

page
95

page
107

page
115

Narrowboats

Most of the boats on the narrow UK canals are based on commercial carrying vessels that transported cargo in the UK as far back as the early eighteenth century. Originally drawn by horse, and then later powered by steam and then diesel engine, the vessels were often worked as a pair, one of the pair being unpowered. An entire family would have lived aboard in a small cabin at the rear of the boat, the rest being cargo space usually covered by cloth to keep the weather out.

Tugs

The purposeful lines of tugboats are very distinctive and their deep, wide hulls lend themselves well to conversion into living accommodation. Most tugs in working condition are dominated by their engine and fuel tanks. Even a large ship of around 80ft (25m) would have relatively small living quarters. However, with the main engine and other machinery removed the space to convert into living accommodation can be huge.

Yachts and Motorsailers

Yachts, large and small, are used as homes in every corner of the globe. Most are built with the primary purpose of sailing, and this can sometimes be at odds with the ideal conditions for living. A large yacht may have fairly small living accommodation – sail storage areas combined with long, narrow bows often reduce the usable living space.

Motorsailers fall somewhere between a motor yacht and a yacht. Designs vary but in most cases the sails are there to supplement the engine and reduce rolling at sea. The hull shape of a motorsailer usually gives greater interior volume compared to a yacht of the same length.

The Practicalities

The high price of housing worldwide has encouraged people to consider other alternatives, and living on the water is an option in many countries. But, if you're thinking seriously about living in a home that floats, you need to make sure you understand some of the practical problems you will face. It is a complex and evolving subject so this book is an overview rather than a definitive guide. There are many organisations that can help you with your research; this book has an accompanying website **www.ahomeafloat.com** which has links to a variety of resources including some of the boats featured.

Cost

Many people are attracted to the idea of living afloat because they see it as a cheaper way of living compared to bricks and mortar, but that isn't likely to be the case. A boat, ship or houseboat may be cheaper to buy than a house, but they are much more difficult to finance for the main reason that it is unlikely for a house to sail off into the sunset. Longer term, they are less likely to increase in value and they require more maintenance, some of which can be quite specialised. It helps if you are a practical person who can tackle the day to day maintenance yourself.

Cruising or static?

The vast array of options for floating homes vary from stationary houseboats to vessels capable of crossing oceans. There are trade-offs with all designs, so you need to think about the kind of living arrangements you need. If the merest ripple of movement makes you reach for a bucket, then a houseboat is likely to be more suitable than a fully fledged ocean-going yacht. All floating homes will move to a degree, and this is part of the charm of living on the water, but a large houseboat on a non-tidal waterway would be very stable.

Moorings

If you plan to stay in one place for any length of time the most important thing to resolve before buying a boat or houseboat is where you are going to moor it. Waterfront land is in great demand for obvious reasons, so you need to be sure you can find somewhere to tie-up the floating home of your dreams, especially if you plan to stay a while.

RIGHT: *The crew of Zwerver wait for the tide to come in before they head for home. See page 64.*

Residential or non-residential?

Moorings fall into two main categories; those that are residential and those that are not. Some of the latter will turn a blind eye to people living afloat, but that doesn't make for a secure way of life if it is your only home. The definition of what is residential will vary, so you need to check with your mooring operator. But if you are spending more than a few nights every week staying on your boat then you are likely to be classed as residential.

Creature comforts

Imagine all of the things you take for granted in a house – endless hot water, a large kitchen filled with gadgets, sumptuous bathrooms, lots of space – you can have them all in a floating home. Sometimes, however, the systems are just a little bit more complicated to achieve the same result.

Heating

A common question non boat dwellers ask is 'Is it cold in winter?' In most cases the answer is no. A properly built houseboat or vessel designed to support living aboard is likely to have a smaller air volume than a house and usually better insulation. A common practice with converted barges in northern Europe is to have the hull sprayed with a layer of polyurethane foam insulation that adheres to the steel. Once the interior is constructed inside this hull you end up with a very thermally efficient dwelling. There are downsides to this smaller air volume in that condensation can be more of a problem, particularly in damp or humid climates, so extra thought needs to be given to ensure adequate ventilation and airflow.

Heating systems

Solid fuel stove

The simplest system you are likely to find is a solid fuel (coal or wood) burning stove. They produce lots of heat but need lots of attention – such as carrying the fuel, cleaning out the ashes – and they don't warm your home in the morning without someone getting out of bed to light it. In British narrowboats it is common to see a small stove that has a water jacket inside that allows it to be connected to a series of radiators to distribute the heat round the boat.

Electric fan heaters and radiators

If your floating home is on a mooring with an electricity supply it is quite feasible to use conventional domestic heaters designed for home use. They can be costly to run but are cheap to purchase. Sometimes boat mooring electricity supplies cannot provide enough current to run a large bank of electric heaters.

Gas heaters

You can use on-board gas cylinders to provide heat from small radiators or stove units. They are fine for short term use but they use a lot of gas, and cylinders can be expensive to refill and heavy to transport. If your floating home has a permanent shore connection you may also have a gas supply which could power a conventional domestic heating system.

Diesel heaters

If your floating home is a diesel powered vessel you can use the same fuel to provide heat. There are several types:

- *Blown air*: a small furnace generates hot air which is vented around the boat through tubing to small outlets. The furnace unit is usually kept in a machine room near the engine and has an exhaust that exits through the hull. They were originally developed as truck cabin heaters so spare parts are readily available, and many units have timers to allow them to switch on automatically at designated times.

ABOVE: A solid-fuel stove is an economical source of heat for many floating homes including Lily. See page 40.

LEFT: *All the comforts of home and the ability to slip away for a weekend's travel. Anna Maria is a large barge with the Dillon family of four living aboard. See page 14.*

- *Drip feed*: a small stove that burns diesel through a drip feed burner. These are very simple and use no electricity so are well suited to a vessel that moves around. The unit is often designed to look like a traditional solid fuel stove and can have a water jacket in the back to run radiators or provide a hot water supply.
- *Diesel furnace*: similar to a domestic system with a diesel fired boiler unit that circulates heated water to a series of radiators around the dwelling. Many people use domestic systems as they are usually cheaper to buy than a marine equivalent. Domestic systems usually require mains voltage electricity to operate, and are perhaps the most sophisticated heating systems, with full control of when they turn on and off just as you would have in a house. A properly set up system is likely to provide hot water as well.

Water

In a house you turn on a tap and water comes out. If you live on a boat this may happen too, but the means of achieving it may require a bit more machinery than you'd find in a house. Vessels designed to travel will usually have large tanks of fresh and waste water stored on board. A freshwater tank has to be filled from a water supply, and a pump or a series of pumps will pressurise the sytem to allow you to turn on a tap and have water when you need it.

A permanently moored vessel may have a shore connection to mains water, and apart from the occasional pipe freezing in cold climates, the system is the same as a domestic one.

Hot water

Water heating systems fall into two main categories:
- *Instantaneous*: a gas powered device to heat water as you need it. This is similar to a domestic system but designed for marine use, using bottled gas instead of mains. As with all gas systems onboard boats, they require proper installation and thorough maintenance to ensure safe operation. They are becoming less popular because of the difficulty in maintaining such systems and keeping them up to scratch with safety inspections.
- *Stored water systems*: a large insulated cylinder stores water until you need it. These are used as part of a heating system, and a variety of heat sources can be used to heat the water, from a dedicated boiler or stove to the main propulsion engine. Cruising boats may also have a device called a colorifier that uses cooling water from the engine to heat hot water for domestic use.

There are other water heating devices found on boats including electric heating elements and solar systems through to a simple kettle on a stove, but a long term liveaboard will need a good reliable system to make life comfortable all year round.

Toilets

Put a group of liveaboard boaters in a room and it won't be long before they are talking about toilets. It is a complex subject and often not as straightforward as the standard systems you will find in houses worldwide. There are many options to choose from:

BELOW: *Quarry, an ex-cargo barge converted into a luxurious houseboat with a garden mooring. See page 80.*

- Small boats built for the sea are likely to have a system known as a sea toilet. All waste discharges directly overboard through an outlet in the hull. They are simple, but prone to blocking up when the wrong things are put into them. You will usually find a notice nearby that says: 'Please do not flush anything that hasn't been eaten first'. If you do, expect to be handed a spanner, rubber gloves and some instructions. Sea toilets are only suited to open water; most countries do not allow their use on rivers or harbours for obvious reasons.
- A permanently moored houseboat is quite likely to have the exact same system as a conventional house: a toilet that is connected to mains sewerage.
- The next most common system you will find is a holding tank to store the sewage until you are ready to dispose of it. The smallest will be like the systems you find in a caravan, and once full can be removed from the boat by hand and emptied at a dedicated point in a marina. If you are living aboard this could become a fairly regular task, so boats designed for habitation will have a large tank permanently fitted that allows several weeks of storage before being emptied by attaching a special hose on the mooring or by another vessel that pulls up alongside. Larger ships may have a combined system that allows discharge overboard when at sea and storage when moored.
- A relative newcomer to the world of marine toilets is the composting toilet. This is a unit that treats the sewage waste by means of dehydration, moisture evaporation and decomposition reducing the amount of final waste to a soil-like compost that can be disposed of occasionally. Their main advantage is they they use very little water.

ABOVE: *A British narrowboat built for the narrow canals is designed to a maximum width of 7ft (2.1m).* Iris No3. *See page 100.*

Electrical systems

A permanently moored vessel is likely to have its power supplied from an external source, usually a cable connecting it to the shore and to the mains grid. Vessels designed for cruising will often have a combination system that allows connection to the shore when power is available and a bank of batteries for when it is not. A generator running from the same fuel as the main engine may also be present to provide power and charge the house batteries. The main propulsion engine will also provide charge for the house batteries while cruising.

Battery power is at a much lower voltage (12v or 24v) and will require a device known as an inverter to allow you to use conventional domestic appliances. The inverter converts the low voltage direct current stored in batteries to mains voltage alternating current required by most appliances.

Wind generators and solar panels can be used to supplement the fossil-fuel powered charging systems, but in most cases the onboard power supply will not be able to supply enough current for heavy draw items like air conditioners or electric heaters.

Downsizing

A large houseboat or barge may offer the same space as a conventional house, but if you are making a move to a boat or even a small ship be prepared to dispose of some of your possessions. You can start with the lawnmower as most moorings won't have any grass to mow. That's not to say

ABOVE: *Bathrooms afloat can be every bit as luxurious as those on land.* Libertijn. *See page 34.*

moorings with private gardens are impossible to find, but they are less likely. The same goes for garages, so if yours is packed to the rafters with accumulated junk you'll need to decide which things you really want to keep and put the rest in storage or sell it.

A lifestyle choice

So far I've mentioned some of the cold, hard realities of living afloat, and if you've never been inside a floating home you may be thinking it is all a bit daunting so here are some of the positive aspects:

- Proximity to water – and the nature that that usually brings – makes many people feel content and happy. There is always something to look at out of the window of a boat, whether it's another boat passing, the ocean, or a family of ducks, it can be more pleasant than the view from many houses or apartments. This can be true even in a large city like London.

- A collection of floating homes moored together is quite likely to bring a whole bunch of diverse people together with a common interest. A good community spirit is almost guaranteed, and you will probably find the answer to those new questions you never thought you'd ask, like 'How do I stop this leak?'.

- Many floating homes give you the option to move around and take all of your belongings with you. Did someone say adventure?

- The ability to change your view if you get tired of it is a reality in a floating home. Even a large houseboat can be craned on to the back of a truck and taken to a completely new city.

ABOVE: *A Dutch barge – the Nova Cura – moored on a picturesque canal in the Netherlands. See Page 56 .*

A note about terminology

We took the decision in this book only to use basic nautical terminology to describe various areas in the featured homes. In many instances standard housing terms were used to avoid confusion. Below is a summary of the terms and their nautical equivalent.

Front of the ship	Bow
Back of the ship	Stern
Kitchen	Galley
Main living area	Saloon
Bedroom	Cabin
Toilet/bathroom	Heads

Barges

RIGHT: *Anna Maria on her mooring at Albion Quay, Wandsworth, London.*

A home afloat

Anna Maria

Chris and Alison Barnes were searching for a home with soul when they moved to London in 1988. They had always liked the idea of living on a boat but it took another seven years until they moved aboard their first ever floating home, a Dutch barge called *Anna Maria*.

She is a traditional Luxemotor design, measuring 82ft (25m) and her home mooring is at Albion Quay on the River Thames in Wandsworth. The youngest members of the Barnes family, Ella (8) and Alfie (6), have only ever known a life on the river.

Alison described the best bits about living afloat, including:

- Feeling the rhythm of the seasons via the river – spotting the first goslings or the first moorhen of Spring, and feeding the swans out of your window just before breakfast on a weekday.

- Coming through the gate to the mooring and the cares of the 'outside' world just melting away!

- Going for a weekend cruise and picnic in our tender.

- Seeing the excitement in the faces of visiting children coming to play with our children.

- A stormy night outside with the sound of the rain and river slapping against the barge but inside the glow of the wood burning stove making everything cosy.

- The smell of burning wood drifting from the chimney on a cold winter's day.

And the worst:

- Battling for space with a family of four and a two-cabin barge. But this in turn leads you to question the amount of 'stuff' you actually need. We work on the principle that you actually only use 20% of your 'stuff' 80% of the time so the rest can be recycled, given to charity or put in storage. She'd also love to have a garden for the children.

At the moment they don't travel in *Anna Maria* except for essential maintenance work, but they have plans for a family cruise to Holland and France in the next few years.

ABOVE AND LEFT:
The Barnes family live within a community of residential boats.

Photography: Alison Wagstaffe

ABOVE: *The main living space.*
RIGHT: *The galley and dining area.*

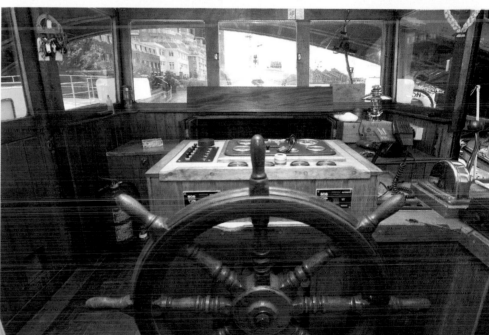

TOP LEFT: *The master bedroom features a raised bed with storage underneath.*

TOP MIDDLE: *The well equipped bathroom.*

TOP RIGHT: *Emergency lighting.*

ABOVE: *The wheelhouse is a nice place to sit and watch the river traffic passing by.*

LEFT: *The children have special bunks with a bed on top and a rumpus room below.*

Apelonia Maria

Amsterdam is the European city most famous for its collection of houseboats and this is where Arie Hoekstra and his wife Gerda live aboard their barge *Apelonia Maria*.

She is a 75ft (27.2m) long traditional type of barge known as a Luxemotor and was built in Alphen aan de Rijn, the Netherlands, in 1913 to transport sand.

Arie and Gerda bought her from a friend of theirs who had lived aboard for nine years previously and embarked on a complete rebuild to bring her up to the stunning condition you see here. The ship was stripped back to a bare hull and a new superstructure built. A much larger wooden cabin was constructed to replace the area where the skipper would originally have steered the ship, and this space now forms a large open plan kitchen and dining area. All the changes were designed by a marine architect to keep the new look sympathetic to her original hull shape.

Apelonia Maria is now permanently moored with normal household services such as gas, water and electricity supplied directly from a shore connection. They have no plans to move around, so the engine was also removed to create extra space.

Cooking and central heating are all powered by gas with an additional log-burning stove in the main living area for cold winters.

Arie and Gerda have lived aboard for four years and chose a life afloat to enable them to live right in the centre of Amsterdam but still maintain a connection with nature thanks to the proximity of the water. Their mooring is also on a busy part of the canal system so there is always something to watch passing by the windows.

TOP: *Apelonia Maria on her mooring in the centre of Amsterdam.*

ABOVE: *Apelonia Maria's mooring in 1900 and in more recent times.*

ABOVE LEFT: *The galley is built into the wheelhouse and retains the original steering wheel.*

ABOVE: *Inside the wheelhouse showing galley and dining area.*

ABOVE: *The interior looking towards the stern.*

LEFT: *The main living area with log-burning stove.*

Photography: Arie Hoekstra

LEFT AND BELOW:
Avontuur on her mooring on the
River Thames in London.

Avontuur

It took nearly five years before Phil Hart found a boat that he felt met all his needs for living aboard. He found *Avontuur* in Vlaardingen, the Netherlands and brought her over to the UK to a mooring in Chertsey, Surrey, on the River Thames, where he now lives aboard. She is a 100ft (30m) long ship of a traditional Dutch design known as a Luxemotor.

She was called *Cornelis* when Phil found her but he reverted to her original name which he preferred – *Avontuur* translates as 'adventure'.

She was built in 1912 and spent most of her life carrying sand until 1966, when the skipper who had worked her for many years bought her and converted her for living aboard. Phil bought *Avontuur* directly from him so he has a good knowledge of her more recent history.

Phil has lived onboard for two years and during that time has refitted much of her interior which was in need of some modernisation. It's not quite finished yet but it's getting close. The skipper's quarters in the stern of the ship are still in their original condition, so Phil plans to restore them to their former glory.

Avontuur can occasionally be seen travelling the upper reaches of the Thames as Phil likes to slip his mooring and go exploring when work permits. She contains everything needed for a life afloat when travelling, thanks to a large generator which can supply enough electricity to power all the ship's systems. She has gas and electric cooking facilities as well as a diesel-fired central heating system.

Phil chose a life afloat because he liked the idea of an alternative lifestyle and doesn't regret his decision for one minute. He loves the tranquility of the river and the community spirit of the other boaters in the area.

Photography: Alison Wagstaffe

ABOVE: *Phil has recently constructed a wooden deck so that he has a nice level space to dine outside if the weather cooperates.*

LEFT: *Engine controls inside the wheelhouse.*

BELOW: *The master bedroom.*

RIGHT: *The galley with a view out onto the river.*

BOTTOM LEFT: *The entrance to the boat leads you into the main living area.*

BOTTOM MIDDLE: *The bathroom.*

BOTTOM RIGHT: *The entrance to the captain's cabin!*

TOP: *The main living area.*

ABOVE: *The stern of the ship retains the original master's cabin from when Avontuur was a working ship.*

Chester

From the outside *Chester* looks like a conventional Luxemotor Dutch barge, but take a step inside and you realise she is a little bit special. The entire interior was custom built in solid teak with the bathroom and galley built from scratch. There are some pretty clever details, including a dining table that is stored in the ceiling, a hand-carved wood and stained-glass bathroom door, and illuminated champagne buckets built into the bedroom cupboards.

Throughout the boat, the attention to detail is amazing: the entire galley is hidden away when not in use and the same fixtures and fittings are used throughout the boat. The bathroom has a very luxurious feel including a double-ended Victorian roll-top bath.

Chester's owner, Marc Salem, is fairly new to the world of floating homes having only been living aboard his 59ft (18m) ship for three months. His mooring is in Chelsea, in the heart of London.

Living afloat represents the end result of a long-held dream for Marc, and for now he is happy to sit on deck and admire the view on a sunny day. However, he does have plans to fire up *Chester's* engine and do some exploring.

ABOVE: *In the bathroom a double-ended Victorian roll-top bath blends nicely with the teak interior panels.*

ABOVE RIGHT: *Neat study area that can fold away when not in use.*

LEFT: *Master bedroom with built-in champagne buckets visible to the right of the photograph.*

TOP LEFT AND FAR LEFT:
The bathroom features a hand carved wooden door with an intricate stained-glass inset.

ABOVE: *A large skylight and lots of large bronze portholes allow plenty of natural light to enter.*

LEFT: *The main living area with stairs to the wheelhouse.*

ABOVE AND RIGHT:
The hand-built galley features all the appliances you need for comfortable living. When not in use everything can be hidden away.

De Jelte

The beginning of a life afloat for Stefan Fritz and Julie Shaughnessy stemmed from a love of water and the outdoors. They spent two years living on a narrowboat on the UK canals and enjoyed the simplicity of the lifestyle. Their interest in boats and boating progressed to the purchase of a larger ship, a 69ft (21m) long 1910 Dutch Beurtschip, and further progressed to a love of traditional sailing ships and the purchase of their current home, an 85ft (26m) long sailing ship called *De Jelte*. She is a traditional Dutch design known as a Klipper.

They bought *De Jelte* in 1998 – the previous owners had completed a lot of the difficult aspects of restoring an old ship, including replacing all of the old steel on the bottom of the hull, installing a better engine, lining the interior and installing water and heating systems, but she had no sailing gear. From 1998-2001 Stefan and Julie worked to restore her back to sail and complete the conversion of the interior. The process involved the help of many friends and an enthusiastic boatyard owner – J Tims & Sons on the Thames in London, where *De Jelte* is currently moored. This involved many trips to the Netherlands, long hours in the workshop and the help of some heavy lifting equipment. August 2001 was the first time *De Jelte* had sailed in 70 years. Julie says:

'The transformation of the ship has brought her alive and when at sail the elegance and beauty of the ship is emphasised. We are now the proud owners of a traditional sailing Klipper and are continuing to restore her. Our plans for *De Jelte* include sailing in the Netherlands and the Baltic, and who knows what the future will bring.'

Since they have owned her Stefan and Julie have been able to trace some of her history. From conversations with the previous owners, Han and Wilma Boekwijt, they tracked down the family Engelaar who had worked and cared for the ship between 1910 and 1963. During this period she was converted from sail to motor to keep up with modernisation. In 1963 she was sold into private ownership to Knil Aareans who used her as a houseboat for a few years in Deest, the Netherlands. After that her history is uncertain before the Boekwijts began to restore her.

The Klipper hull shape developed during the nineteenth century when the canals and rivers formed the backbone of the Netherlands' inland transport system. Iron-hulled river Klippers were modelled on the sea-going clippers in the tea trade. Most ships like *De Jelte* carried commercial cargo until after the war and were generally owned by individual skippers. Industrialisation and modernisation in shipping meant that sails were replaced by engines, and larger faster vessels replaced the smaller ships, or the smaller ones were lengthened. Many of the traditional ships were sold for scrap or survived as empty hulls or houseboats. The restoration of these ships by enthusiasts has been growing since the 1970s.

TOP: De Jelte *sailing in 2001.*
ABOVE: De Jelte *in 1952 as a working vessel.*

Photography: Katharine Tolladay

TOP AND RIGHT: *De Jelte's restored galley retains a warm look in keeping with the style of the ship.*

ABOVE: *De Jelte runs before the wind.*

ABOVE: *The main living area features lots of traditional timber panelling.*

FAR LEFT: *The dining area.*

LEFT: *One of the ship's bedrooms.*

ABOVE AND TOP LEFT: De Jelte's bathroom features lots of polished wood and nautical details.

LEFT: The main living area.

Harmonie II

No matter what the weather, you'll find Roger and Sue Biddle aboard *Harmonie II*. She has been their home since retiring two years ago and leaving the UK to begin a new life of adventure cruising on the European waterways. Roger is a former marine engineer so they felt this would be an activity they could manage technically and financially.

They don't have a permanent home mooring and spend the warmer months travelling before finding a different spot to spend the winter. So far they have explored a fair portion of Belgium, Holland and Northern France.

Harmonie II is a 78ft (24m) long Dutch-built Luxemotor barge. She was constructed in 1918 and converted from a cargo vessel into a pleasure craft in 1992. She is extremely well equipped for her life of adventure, including a variety of extras for comfortable cruising such as pin anchors (pointed steel poles that extend through the hull to the river or canal bed) at the front and rear of the ship and even a hydraulic crane to lift a small car onto the deck.

Roger and Sue described what they liked about their cruising life:

- A different place every night if you want.
- Camaraderie amongst the barging community.
- Ever-changing scenery.
- The ability to moor up in the centre of Europe's great cities in luxury accommodation for a fraction of the price of an equivalent hotel.
- Entertaining friends and family when cruising.

And the things they find a challenge:

- Missing out on friends and family social life.
- Keeping up with news from home.
- Not being able to find good English beef and free range meat.
- Clothes shopping, finding fresh water and good moorings on the Seine.

ABOVE: *Starting out their crusing life in Belgium brought some challenging weather.*

LEFT: *The good life, moored in Ool, Belgium.*

Photography: Roger Biddle

ABOVE: *The bathroom.*

LEFT: *The main living area features a real brick wall — the bricks help to serve as ballast.*

BELOW LEFT: *The galley.*

BELOW: *The guest bedroom.*

BOTTOM LEFT: *The crane in action, lifting Roger and Sue's small car onto the stern deck.*

Libertijn of Alphen

Emma Blackburn and Don Galles wanted to buy a house in France for their retirement but couldn't decide where they wanted to live, so they built a luxury floating home instead that allows them to keep their options open and move around. That home is *Libertijn*, an 83ft (25.4m) long ship of a traditional Dutch design known as a Klipperaak. She is pictured here in St Katharine's Dock on the River Thames, London while en-route to her first summer in France.

Libertijn was built in 1910 in the Netherlands as a sailing cargo vessel. An engine and wheelhouse were added in 1920, and at some point in the 1970s she was shortened and converted for living aboard. Don and Emma bought her in 1999 and embarked on an extensive refit that took five years.

The ship has a large split-level open-plan area just forward of the wheelhouse that comprises the galley and the main living area. Emma and Don wanted this area to be both modern and functional, deliberately avoiding traditional ship styling, opting instead for bright colours and natural woods set against stainless steel and polished granite.

A wood-burning stove is a small concession to traditionalism and makes for cosy winter nights but a sophisticated central heating and air conditioning system maintains perfect internal conditions regardless of the outside temperature.

Hi-tech systems abound aboard *Libertijn*; in addition to all the electronic systems required for safe navigation, Don installed a cinema and sound system that would put many commercial theatres to shame. At the flick of a switch a projector rises from the coffee table and a screen drops to cover the forward wall.

The ship has two cabins for guests, one with a queen-sized bed for couples, and one with two single beds. Behind the wheelhouse is the master cabin, sited where the original living quarters were when *Libertijn* was a working boat. During the refit all of the oak panels and teak surrounds from

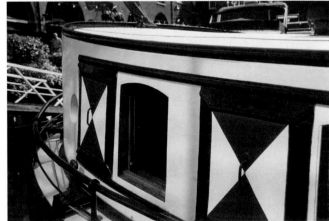

TOP AND RIGHT: Libertijn *moored in St Katharine's Dock en-route to France.*

ABOVE: Libertijn's *stern cabin has traditionally painted storm shutters.*

Photography: Katharine Tolladay

OF ALPHEN

the 1920s original were dismantled and refurbished. They were then reinstalled into a new configuration to change a three-room living area into a single large bedroom housing a queen-size bed and a two metre marble bath. The interior has been carefully designed to reflect the art deco feeling of the 1920s. Even the speakers were custom-built using solid teak that had been French polished to match the walls.

Both Don and Emma love to cook, so the galley features a commercial six burner gas hob, a large commercial gas oven (both powered by bottled gas), two refrigerators, freezer, ice maker, dish washer, warming drawer and granite worktops.

Since completing the refit Don and Emma have done quite a lot of cruising aboard *Libertijn*. Don says:

'Before May 2004 we made several trips up and down the Thames – as far as Henley-on-Thames and even participated in the 2003 Thames Traditional Boat Rally. In April 2004 we

ABOVE RIGHT AND BELOW: *The main living area with a wood-burning stove; a small concession to traditionalism.*

ABOVE: *Entrance to the main living area.*

spent a month at St Katharine's Dock in London, then crossed the English Channel – entering the canal system at Calais. Once on the European continent, we spent a few weeks touring Belgium (including Bruges and Ghent), and then toured the Champagne and Burgundy regions of France. This winter we are in Auxerre, near Chablis in northern Burgundy.

'We plan to tour a different area of the European continent each summer, spending each winter in a different location. Next spring we are considering Alsace. We will eventually go all the way down to the Mediterranean, and all the way up through Belgium, Holland and Germany, and are entertaining thoughts of Eastern Europe.'

Don and Emma chose a life afloat because they have always enjoyed boating, even though they did not buy their first boat until 1998. They still own that boat now and keep her on the Thames – she is a 1960s wooden Star Craft cruiser called *Lady Bea*.

'At the time, cruising our wooden boat on the Thames was the only respite to otherwise crushing jobs. We had moved to England from America and were living in rented accommodation, so buying a boat to live on didn't sound unreasonable, especially since we were not planning to stay in the UK long-term. That was the beginning of a slippery slope, and what started as an experiment to live on water while in the UK became a passion. We have gone from boring live-to-work computer industry types to vagabond gypsies,

travelling the European waterways with reckless abandon.' Don loves it so much he is writing a book documenting their adventures aboard *Libertijn*.

'Living afloat enables you to combine a constantly changing environment with the comforts of home. When you wake, the view out your window is fresh to your eyes. The town or city awaits your exploration. There are local specialities to sample, customs to experience, languages to learn, and people to get to know. At the end of each day you can retire to a comfortable, familiar environment with your own kitchen to cook in and bed to sleep in. The following day you can further explore this area, or start the engine and go somewhere new. Because you always return to your comfortable home, you do not get travel weary or homesick. Because your environment is constantly changing, you are never bored – in fact, the increased stimulus makes your mind more active, and constant exposure to new people and places broadens your thinking.

'The novelty factor of living aboard a boat should not be underestimated. It provides an immediate talking point with the locals you meet. Your friends and relatives are much more interested in visiting you. Old friends may think you have gone slightly mad, but they all harbour some hidden admiration for your unconventional lifestyle. Other boaters you meet tend to be slightly eccentric – just as you have become, and mutual understanding of the madness that this type of lifestyle requires always makes for impromptu parties.

ABOVE: *The galley features commercial grade appliances and a bright, modern colour scheme.*

RIGHT AND FAR RIGHT: *The guest bathroom is fitted in quality materials.*

LEFT: *The wheelhouse looking forward from the steering position.*

RIGHT: *The bathroom in the master bedroom.*

BELOW: *The master bedroom. The wooden panelling was salvaged from the original master's cabin, refurbished and installed into a new layout.*

'Piloting a large vessel through narrow waterways presents its own challenges, but traffic jams and road rage are not among them. From your aquatic vantage point, you often see cars queued up – usually because the bridge they want to cross has lifted to let you through. Not only do waterways often afford views that are not available from roads there is a sheer joy to skippering a boat that is impossible to describe to the uninitiated. Perversely, large craft that present a challenge to the skipper can be the most fun.

'I have always hated packing for a holiday. You inevitably forget important items, your suitcase is stuffed to bursting point, you are over the weight limit at the airline desk. Living afloat, you do not pack. You do not forget important items. You can buy cases of wine and have room to store them. You have all your favourite clothes, music, food, drink, movies, etc with you at all times.

'On a boat you are responsible for systems you always took for granted in a house – supplying pressurised water, generating electricity, disposing of effluent. In addition, most houses do not have a central engine the size of a large sofa to contend with. As a result, you learn to be an electrician, plumber, mechanic, and decorator. I now laugh at the things that used to daunt me when I lived in a house. You might think that this is one of the 'worst' bits about living afloat, but after the initial frustration I have found I enjoy the challenges. Most other people who live on boats find the same strange appeal – attend a party with boaters and have the host mention a nagging system problem they are having, and minutes later the floorboards will be up while four different people have an enthusiastic go at fixing it.'

Lily

Buying a barge enabled Alison Alderton and Roger Harrington to combine their respective passions – travel and boating. The couple had shared many boating holidays together and initially bought *Lily* to use during weekends and holidays. They soon found that just weekends onboard were not enough so they decided to sell their house and move onboard full time.

Alison is a travel and inland waterways writer and feels very lucky that she gets to combine work with pleasure.

Lily is a 48ft (14.6m) replica Dutch barge built by Sagar Marine in 1996. Alison and Roger bought her in 2005 and since then have logged around 1000 hours of travelling time. They have a permanent mooring in Newark-on-Trent, Nottingham but like to spend as much time as possible travelling. Alison says:

'We like the safety and security of our marina but love to be on the move especially in the autumn and winter months when the waterways are quieter and the birdlife is great. Lily is so warm and cosy inside during these months that it is a real joy to be onboard her.

'The whole point of living on *Lily* was and still is to travel, that's what we think a boat is for. This summer we have been cruising for three months, which involved taking *Lily* across the Wash, our first sea going venture with her, to the waterways of the Fens. Our long term plans are to take *Lily* to the French waterways.

'My favourite item on *Lily* is our solid-fuel stove and the satisfying feeling of finding free wood to burn and free food, such as blackberries, plums, apples and mushrooms. It is such a feeling of achievement to source your own fuel and food.'

Alison and Roger have all the equipment they need for a comfortable life when cruising; generator, power inverter and central heating but the one thing they find annoying is poor television reception. Roger finds it particularly frustrating, as it is always him clambering on the roof trying to adjust the aerial in the pouring rain!

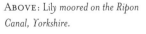

ABOVE: *Lily moored on the Ripon Canal, Yorkshire.*

RIGHT: *Moored while the rain passes during one of Lily's many trips on the British canal network.*

Photography: Alison Alderton

ABOVE: *The master bedroom with built-in wardrobes.*

MIDDLE: *Lily's bathroom is off the main bedroom.*

RIGHT: *The guest bedroom is in the stern of the ship.*

LEFT: *The galley and open-plan living area with solid-fuel stove for heating.*

ABOVE: *The main living area showing the stairs to the wheelhouse.*

Lobelia

A small island on the Thames is how the owners of this ex-commercial barge jokingly describe their home. They are not far wrong; at 127ft (39m) *Lobelia* is certainly one of the larger vessels to feature in this book.

Lobelia was built in Belgium in 1962 and is a traditonal type of vessel known as a Spitz. She is now home to Andy Bailey, Siobhan Tucker and their two children Danny (5) and Callum (3). They have lived aboard for two years but previously lived on a smaller barge for seven years. They started living afloat as an experiment to see if they liked it and have never looked back. Andy and Siobhan converted *Lobelia* from an empty hull and incorporated all of the things they needed in a floating home based on living in their previous barge. *Lobelia* spent 18 months in a boatyard having steelwork built, bow thruster, generator, portholes, crane, and 80 tons of old railway track as ballast fitted before the interior conversion even started. The layout now features a double bedroom/play room with an en-suite shower and toilet in the original skipper's cabin at the stern. There are two other double rooms which are linked by a sliding door to make a large room for the boys, a main double bedroom towards the bow with en-suite shower and toilet, and a separate family bathroom.

Their home mooring is at Penton Hook Marina on the River Thames near Chertsey, Surrey and they are neighbours to *Avontuur* also featured in this book (see page 20).

Although *Lobelia* is fully mobile, Andy and Siobhan don't travel in her thanks to work and school pressure. When the children are older, however, they want to take an extended trip through the French waterways.

The things the family love are being in touch with the local wildlife and being aware of the changing seasons as well as the great community that exists. The downside is the cost and availability of a suitable mooring for such a large vessel.

Top: *The imposing bows of* Lobelia.

Above: *The children have a very large deck to play on which has a synthetic grass covering. A wire fence surrounds the area for safety.*

Right: Lobelia *on her home mooring.*

Photography: Alison Wagstaffe

TOP LEFT AND ABOVE: Lobelia has several levels including a raised galley with large windows to enjoy the view. From the galley there are steps up to the wheelhouse.

LEFT: The main living area.

FAR LEFT: *Long corridors in Lobelia.*

LEFT: *Wood fired stove in the main living area.*

BELOW: *The boys' bedroom and play room.*

TOP AND TOP RIGHT: *The master bedroom with en-suite bathroom.*

BOTTOM AND RIGHT: *The guest bedroom with its own bathroom.*

TOP: *Longfellow on her home mooring in Putney.*

TOP RIGHT: *The main living area.*

Longfellow

Home to Simon and Jane Beaufoy, their daughter Ellen and Stanley the cat, *Longfellow* is a 126ft (37.8m) Luxemotor Dutch barge moored at Putney on the River Thames in London. The family have lived onboard for over eight years.

Longfellow was built in Rotterdam to carry grain on the rivers and canals of Europe. She was brought over from the Netherlands during the 1980s. Simon and Jane bought her in a partially converted state and spent several years fitting out the cargo hold to the beautiful condition you see here.

She retains her original skipper's quarters in the stern of the ship, now used as an office and spare bedroom. The main living area is an impressive open-plan space with lots of natural light and a log-burning stove for cosy winter nights. The galley flows through to an open air deck space with shower. A glass roof slides open to keep the garden watered and let the sun shine through.

A diesel-fired range in the galley provides ample heat for cooking and drives radiators throughout the barge for heating. Diesel also powers the main engine; fuel is delivered directly to the barge by river. Simon is keen to use river-based suppliers to help keep commercial traffic alive on the Thames.

Simon and Jane's friends are often picked up from the tube station by ship's tender and travel up-river to *Longfellow* for dinner.

Simon has recently completed the necessary qualifications to handle a barge this size on the Continent, and in the next few years they plan to slip their mooring, head down the Thames and spend a summer or two cruising the European waterways.

Photography: Gary Cookson

MIDDLE LEFT: *The bedroom leads through to the deck area with mini garden and sliding roof.*

LEFT AND ABOVE: *The bathroom and bedroom.*

ABOVE: *Clever details like this porthole window close to the waterline allow you to watch the river go by.*

RIGHT: *The main living area.*

LEFT: *The open air deck space contains a shower with a coil radiator for warmth.*

CENTRE LEFT AND BELOW: *The galley with diesel-fired range.*

LEFT: *The galley flows through to the open air deck.*

Lucia

Mike and Jill Cullen are the most recent in a long line of caring owners of this classic Luxemotor Dutch barge. Unlike other new boat owners who need to carry out a fair bit of investigative work to piece together a history of their vessel, Mike and Jill were delighted to be handed a complete written history of the barge. This detailed previous owners, journeys taken, and maintenance work completed, dating back to when she was built in Stadskanaal, the Netherlands in 1925. They are continuing the process by documenting their ownership.

They have been around small ships for many years, having previously owned a variety of narrowboats and a smaller Dutch barge which they lived on during a house move. They decided they liked it so much that they had to find a larger barge to make their permanent home. *Lucia* is 79ft (24m) long and their home mooring is at Bell Weir Lock on the River Thames. They have lived afloat since 2005.

They like to keep *Lucia* moving with several trips a year up and down the Thames. They are planning some more extended trips in the near future.

Mike and Jill described the best bits about living afloat, including:

- The feeling of freedom living on the water gives you.
- Being able to watch the wildlife.
- The ability to take your home and possessions with you without having to pack a bag.
- The wonderful social life enjoyed with other boat people, particularly members of the Barge Association.

And the worst:

- Finding somewhere to pump out the black tank!

FAR LEFT: *Lucia on her home mooring.*

TOP: *The forward deck is a great area to sit out and watch the river going by.*

ABOVE: *The wheelhouse forms a useful extra room when not travelling.*

BOTTOM LEFT: *Lucia on Beale Park lake.*

TOP: *The galley with stairs to the wheelhouse.*

TOP RIGHT: *The main living area.*

BELOW: *Mike and Jill's antique furniture blends nicely with Lucia's interior style.*

RIGHT: *The dining area.*

TOP LEFT AND ABOVE: *The master bedroom.*

TOP RIGHT: *The main bathroom.*

Mirage

David and Mary Heath have owned a variety of different boats dating back over 30 years so when it came to building a new boat to live aboard they had some very specific requirements. For a start, they wanted the styling to reflect the lines of a classic Dutch barge but in a newly built ship. They designed *Mirage* to maximise the interior space while keeping the exterior dimensions within the 60ft by 12ft 6in (18.3m by 3.8m) maximum required to comfortably cruise the English widebeam waterways.

They managed to squeeze a lot into *Mirage's* accommodation including; a cloakroom, store, large galley, breakfast bar, saloon, bathroom, and two bedrooms – both of which have large built-in wardrobes. David designed a special aluminium folding wheelhouse with a one-piece roll off roof and semicircular leather seating.

The only fuel they have on board is diesel which powers the main engine, generator and central heating. All domestic applicances are electric with a ceramic hob, two multicook microwave ovens, fridge, two freezers, air conditioner, dishwasher, washing machine and dryer.

David and Mary have lived onboard for 18 months since retiring and chose a life afloat to enable them to spend more time cruising the English waterways and cut out the time they spent maintaining their house. They plan to spend the summers cruising and winters on their home mooring at Ratcliffe on Soar, Nottinghamshire, UK.

They described the best aspects to life afloat as the great views and freedom to go cruising when it suits them best. The negative aspects included having to downsize from a large house and having to plan carefully where everything is stored onboard.

ABOVE: Mirage *moored on the Erewash Canal.*

LEFT: *Cruising on the river Trent.*

Photography: David Heath

ABOVE AND LEFT: *The galley is all electric with power supplied by generator and battery storage when cruising.*

LEFT: *The main living area.*

BELOW: *Inside the wheelhouse showing the semicircular leather seating.*

Nova Cura

ife aboard the *Nova Cura* is a truly international experience. Colin Goddard and Danielle Jacobs were born in the UK and USA respectively, and live aboard their Dutch barge in the Netherlands. She is 126ft (38.54m) long traditional Luxemotor design, built in 1928, and their home mooring is in Haringvliet Harbour, Rotterdam.

They have lived onboard since 2004, having undertaken an extensive rebuild that incorporated as many of the original art-deco features of the ship as possible. The cargo hold has been converted into their home and office, and the original skipper's cabin at the stern of the ship has been fully restored.

Colin and Danielle had both been enthusiastic sailors for over ten years before meeting someone by chance who lived aboard an historic ship in Gouda. From that moment they were hooked and had to find a ship of their own. Colin says:

'Rebuilding *Nova Cura* has allowed us, as foreigners, to understand more fully the history and culture of the Netherlands. Dealing with craftsmen has also improved our Dutch significantly. There is a lovely community of people on the water. People help each other and are friendly, without being intrusive.

'Life on the water is always interesting – ships passing, tide changing, water birds flying and swimming around us.'

The *Nova Cura* has had a very interesting life. During the Second World War, she and her skipper were forced to work for the occupying German forces, transporting sand and gravel for various building projects. Towards the end of 1944, with the Allies approaching from the south, the skipper of the *Nova Cura* (or *Bertha* as she was called then) chose to sink his ship in the Donge River, near Raamsdonksveer, in order to prevent it falling into the hands of the retreating German army. She lay semi-submerged for the remaining six months of the war. After the liberation of the Netherlands, the ship was refloated and refitted. The skipper continued to work her until handing her over to his son in 1955.

TOP: *The* Nova Cura *— moored on a picturesque canal in the Netherlands during one of Colin and Danielle's many trips.*

ABOVE: *Sunset on the Nedrrijn River.*

ABOVE RIGHT: *The original skipper's cabin was restored during the rebuild.*

Photography: Colin Goddard

TOP RIGHT: *The main living area.*

ABOVE: *The master bedroom.*

MIDDLE: *The galley.*

RIGHT: *The wheelhouse.*

Vrijheid

reedom is the English translation of *Vrijheid* and it is the feeling of freedom and mobility that a life afloat gives the owners of this classic ship. Bruce and Caroline Le Gros are both New Zealanders but have lived in the UK for the last 20 years, 12 of those aboard *Vrijheid*. She is currently moored at Chiswick Pier on the River Thames, London, which has visitor and residential moorings.

Vrijheid is 92ft (28m) long and built to a traditional Dutch design known as a Stijlsteven. During her working life she traded between Holland and Germany on the River Rhine carrying bulk food products and general cargo until she retired in 1952. She was converted to living accommodation in the years that followed, and Bruce and Caroline bought her in 1993 and sailed her from the Netherlands to the UK. They have upgraded and modernised her interior and systems over the years so that they now own a luxurious and historically important ship.

Vrijheid is to be seen regularly on the river; her owners require little excuse to slip their moorings and head off on an adventure. They have taken her as far upstream as her size will allow – Dorchester on Thames – as well as regular trips to Whitstable and Faversham Creek at the mouth of the Thames.

Bruce and Caroline initially chose a life afloat because they had a dream to buy a yacht and sail home to New Zealand. They bought a barge to see if they found the life agreeable and so far they love it.

'We live in London on the water for a fraction of the cost of our land-locked neighbours, coupled with the ability to slip away for a break without needing to even pack a toothbrush.'

TOP LEFT: Vrijheid *underway on the River Thames.*
TOP: *Engine controls.*
BOTTOM: Vrijheid *on her home mooring.*

Photography: Katharine Tolladay

LEFT: *The formal dining area.*
TOP: *The living area.*
ABOVE: *Beautiful antique lamps add to the historic feel of the ship's interior.*

ABOVE: *The stern of* Vrijheid *with her tender ready to be launched.*

ABOVE MIDDLE: *Ship's stores.*

ABOVE RIGHT: *Galley details.*

RIGHT: *The guest bedroom.*

FAR RIGHT: *The galley features a traditional stove that is powered by kerosene (paraffin).*

TOP: *The main living area.*

ABOVE: *Keeping an eye on the weather.*

FAR LEFT: *The wheelhouse features lots of traditional timber detailing, adding to the feeling of warmth.*

LEFT: *The imposing bows of Vrijheid.*

Barges ～ 61

Yavanna

Imagine the excitement of discovering a picturesque little village around the next river bend, exploring the countryside by bicycle or cruising right into the centre of a lovely, historic European city in your own floating home. Australians Max and Vicki Cooper decided to turn this excitement into a way of life after hiring a boat on the French canals in 2002 during a holiday.

Retiring three years later the couple turned their holiday romance with boats into a more permanent relationship when they bought *Yavanna,* a 58ft (17.5m) long replica Dutch barge built by Pickwell and Arnold in the UK in 1996.

Yavanna's original owner was a cabinet maker and wood turner who handcrafted the boat's interior from cherrywood and cedar. Featuring superb attention to detail, the roomy interior includes 38 bevelled glass panes in the fixed cabinetry and etched glass panels in the bedroom and bathroom doors. She also has a carved four poster bed, with a huge hatch and ladder in the bedroom for views and ventilation. A cosy atmosphere is created by an antique pot belly stove which provides heat to supplement their diesel-fired central heating.

Yavanna has a demountable wheelhouse for low bridges, and her own little crane to lift the roof off should the need arise. With Max in the wheelhouse and Vicki 52ft (16m) away on the bow, the couple usually cruise with the front window down, communicating by walkie-talkie or hand signals when negotiating tricky moorings.

The boat's engine has an interesting history. It was manufactured shortly after the Second World War for the British Admiralty and kept unused in storage until 1996 when it was sold and fitted to *Yavanna.*

With their liveaboard lifestyle of no stress, excellent food and wine, and meeting interesting people every step of the way, the couple intend to travel the 8500 km of navigable inland waterways in France before setting their sights on Belgium, Holland and Germany.

Photography: Vicki Cooper

FAR LEFT: *Moored for lunch on the Canal du Midi.*

TOP LEFT: *The traditional-style wooden interior makes for a cosy ambience.*

TOP RIGHT: *Yavanna moored at Mèze on the Étang de Thau.*

LEFT: *The unique galley was handcrafted from cherrywood and cedar.*

BOTTOM LEFT: *The master bedroom features a large hatch for ventilation and views.*

BOTTOM MIDDLE: *The fixed cabinets feature 38 bevelled glass panes.*

BOTTOM RIGHT: *The bedroom and bathroom doors feature etched glass panels.*

Zwerver

The Meijers family – Frank, his wife Jacqueline, their son Zimmie, daughter Zegna and Isabel the Rottweiler – live aboard *Zwerver* in the Ertshaven in Amsterdam, the Netherlands. They have lived aboard since 1996.

Zwerver is a type of vessel known as a Klipperaak and has had an interesting past. She was built in 1911 as a sailing cargo vessel and was originally 86ft (26.4m) long. In 1938 she was lengthened to 98ft (30m) and a 2 cylinder 40hp Kromhout diesel engine was added. She was further extended in the 1960s to 125ft (38m) and a larger engine fitted. All of this work enabled her to carry more cargo and extend her working life. She finally retired in 1993 and has been a houseboat ever since.

The Meijers bought her in 1997 and spent several years converting her into a luxury floating home. She is extremely well-equipped, boasting everything from a teak bathroom with sauna to a full workshop including a lathe and milling machine.

Frank and Jacqueline like to travel regularly, so *Zwerver* is a fully functioning ship with a diesel generator to provide electricity when away from the shore.

They chose a life afloat because they like the absence of neighbours and the freedom they are afforded by being able to move whenever they feel like it. *Zwerver* is a very large ship so they also have a lot more space than they would have in a house of the same price. Their home mooring is in a great location in the centre of Amsterdam but is very quiet with great views.

Frank's only complaints are the price of diesel that they use to heat the boat and the water supply from the shore freezing in winter.

ABOVE LEFT: *Zwerver moored at Zwarte Water during one of the family's summer trips.*

ABOVE RIGHT: *Zwerver on her home mooring in Amsterdam.*

TOP RIGHT AND FAR RIGHT: *The main living area has lots of skylights in the roof to give it a bright, spacious feel.*

RIGHT: *The galley aboard Zwerver is very well equipped.*

BOTTOM RIGHT: *The bathroom features marble and polished timber.*

Photography: Frank Meijers

Top left: *The wheelhouse — all controls are within easy reach of the helmsman.*

Top right: *The entrance to the main living area features a special door with custom engraved glass.*

Above: *Zwerver also has a sauna.*

Above right: *The onboard workshop is very well equipped and includes a lathe and milling machine.*

Right: *Jacqueline and Isabel the Rottweiler wait for the tide during one of the family's trips*

Houseboats

Another Story

B ill and Lee Austin have spent most of their adult years living on boats and floating homes of all shapes and sizes. For 15 years they lived aboard a historically important Albacore tuna fishing vessel working all over the north eastern Pacific and raised four children on it.

Their current home is called *Another Story* and they live in Victoria, British Columbia, Canada. It was designed by architect Mark Ankenman and built by International Marine Floatation Systems (IMF) in 1983. Bill and Lee have owned it for six years. They live in Westbay Marine Village which caters specifically to floating homes and liveaboard boaters.

British Columbia has a long history of people living and doing business from floating structures thanks to its fishing and logging industry. What started as a low cost style of urban living has been developed into a sophisticated and well regulated way of life.

The floating part of the house is a large concrete base, designed to be maintenance free and outlast the superstructure. Movement is controlled by steel piles driven into the seabed. Electricity, water, gas and sewage are all connected directly to the dockside.

Another Story's superstructure is constructed from timber and measures 35ft x 40ft (10.7m x 12.1m). It is three storeys tall with open decks all round on the first and second level. The builder had a warehouse filled with wooden beams that needed to be put to use. The architect used this as an idea and designed a modern, rustic house that on the outside has just a hint of Mississippi steamboat.

Bill and Lee saw their move to a floating home as a natural transition from their life on boats and love the sense of space that being so close to the water gives them.

LEFT AND BELOW: *Another Story at Westbay Marine Village.*

Photography: Steve Rosset

ABOVE AND RIGHT: *The kitchen on the second level features exposed timber beams.*

LEFT AND TOP LEFT: *A spiral staircase takes you to the third level.*

ABOVE: *The guest bedrooms and study.*

FAR LEFT: *The master bedroom with suspended bed.*

LEFT AND BELOW LEFT: *The bathroom with glass bricks for light and privacy.*

BELOW: *A substantial wooden staircase takes you up to the second level.*

Greenwood Houseboat

You could say that Wayne Greenwood knows his floating home inside and out. He ought to, having designed and built it himself twice – a freak plumbing accident burned the place down when it was almost finished first time around.

It all started with the outrageous cost of land in the San Francisco Bay area, California. His original plan was to renovate an abandoned warehouse, but the land the warehouse stood on was prohibitively expensive. The conceptual solution to the problem of land cost was simple: build a house that doesn't require land. The execution was a bit trickier, but Wayne likes a challenge.

Wayne enlisted the help of an architect Larick Alan Hill and a builder Arny Messersmith and began construction with a floating concrete hull measuring 42ft x 20ft (12.8m x 6.1m). This was built by a specialist and towed across to Wayne's mooring by tugboat. Wayne leased a plot of water in Docktown Marina, Redwood City, California and took two years to complete the build on-site.

The concrete hull forms the basement which houses Wayne's soundproof recording studio with a two-storey house built on top. The house is 21ft (6.4m) tall.

Wayne and his wife Kelly have lived onboard for over eight years and describe the best bits about living afloat as the water view, the food chain outside the window, the cool breeze, random boats cruising in your backyard, and never having to mow the lawn.

And the worst is that big storms can rock the house a bit more than you'd like, and guests occasionally say cheesy stuff like, 'Permission to come aboard?' and 'Ahoy, matey!' When this happens they usually make them walk the plank.

TOP LEFT AND TOP RIGHT: *Wayne is a keen musician so construction began with a soundproof recording studio in the basement.*

ABOVE: *Family photos.*

LEFT: *The kitchen and dining area.*

Photography: Wayne Greenwood

RIGHT: *The open-plan living area and kitchen are on the first floor.*

LEFT: *The first floor has a suspended walkway to reach the outdoor deck area.*

BELOW: *The master bedroom.*

BELOW LEFT: *The bathroom with industrial finishes.*

Lindelij

A modern houseboat is how Hilleke Koot and Mijndert van der Poel describe their floating home. *Lindelij* was designed by an architect and built in Leiden, the Netherlands in 2002. It was tailor-made to the owners' specifications.

The main living area features lots of natural light thanks to the floor to ceiling windows facing out on to the water. The kitchen and dining area are split over two levels with the bedrooms below.

Hilleke and Mijndert live on board with their dog Boelie on a permanent mooring in Leiden in a community of other houseboats. They have lived afloat for over ten years. The design incorporates all of their best ideas from those years living in different floating homes.

It is a type of vessel known in the Netherlands as an Woonark and is based on a floating concrete pontoon varying between 10in (26cm) in the middle and 7in (18cm) at the edge. The superstructure is constructed from wood and steel and she is permanently connected to mains sewerage, gas and electricity. The main advantage of this type of construction compared to steel is that *Lindelij* does not need to be lifted out of the water for periodic inspections. The concrete base is maintenance free.

Lindelij has a fully equipped kitchen, gas central heating with radiators throughout, and an antique Norwegian wood-burning stove for cosy winter nights.

Hilleke and Mijndert love living afloat because of their proximity to the water and the constantly changing scenery at their door. They also have a small boat moored outside which they use for short trips around the local canals.

Photography: Mijndert van der Poel and John Voermans

TOP LEFT: Lindelij *on her home mooring.*

MIDDLE AND TOP: *The main living area with a view out on to the water.*

MIDDLE LEFT: *The bathroom.*

BOTTOM LEFT: Lindelij *being towed by tugboat to her home mooring.*

TOP RIGHT: *The galley in use.*

RIGHT: Lindelij *viewed from the land.*

FAR RIGHT: *The kitchen and dining area.*

Quarry

The owners of this unique floating home both have families with a history of living on boats so when Stuart Hatton and Stephanie Asplin first started looking for a home together, a houseboat was their first choice.

Quarry is a beautifully restored and converted 1905 Braby and Son's Thames lighter – a type of unpowered vessel used to transport cargo on the River Thames in London.

She is 79ft (24m) long and is one of only a handful of this type of vessel still in existence. Stuart and Stephanie have a fully documented workbook from her period as a cargo vessel dating back over 100 years, detailing all work ever completed on her, and a photographic history of all the work undertaken in more recent years to convert her into living accomodation.

The layout features a master bedroom at the forward end of the vessel plus a second bedroom at the opposite end. There is a 40ft (12.2m) long open-plan living area and throughout the boat are large skylights in the roof which allow lots of natural light in.

Quarry's mooring is at Northolt on the Grand Union Canal, just north of London, and is set in a community of other liveaboard vessels. They even have a garden alongside the boat.

Stuart and Stephanie have lived aboard for 3 years and both have very hectic careers so the relaxed lifestyle and peaceful mooring are a big plus. They love being able to open the skylight of their bedroom in the morning and listen to the ducks and moorhens splashing nearby.

The things they don't like are emptying the toilet regularly, changing gas cyclinders, and having to heat the boat solely from a coal burner.

ABOVE: Quarry *on her mooring.*
LEFT: *The original anchor and machinery have been preserved.*

LEFT: *Deck skylights allow lots of natural light to flood in.*

BELOW LEFT: *The bathroom.*

BELOW: *The master bedroom with ceiling skylight open.*

RIGHT: *A coal burning stove heats the main living space and powers radiators in other parts of the boat.*

FAR RIGHT: *The galley.*

BELOW: *The main living area.*

Strobl Houseboat

When Heinz Strobl retired he was looking for the perfect waterfront property so he bought an old houseboat on the eastern shore of Lake Union, Seattle, USA. His renovation plans proved a little too ambitious for the existing structure so he commissioned architect Gene Morris of Lagerquist & Morris to design him a new one and International Marine Floatation Systems (IMF) to build it.

The end result is a stylish, high-quality floating home that utilises every inch of space. There are two-storeys with a basement – including a 3ft (1m) diameter viewing window underwater. The key to all this is a concrete floating platform which is completely maintenance free. The superstructure of the house is built on top.

The home's focal points are its two-storey wall of wood-framed windows overlooking Lake Union and its barrel-vaulted roof. This shape – that reflects historic Lake Union houseboats – allowed Morris to squeeze every inch out of the 16ft (4.8m) height limit the site imposed and allowed the second floor to have four small decks – one on each corner. High-quality finishes, such as heated bamboo and stone floors, were used throughout.

IMF built the house in Canada and transported it down to Seattle by water. Moving it into its mooring is a story in itself about cooperation by all the neighbours in outboard floating homes who had to be cut loose and floated out into the lake to allow Heinz's home to move in. Moving in was an all day process of high anxiety for the people whose homes were floated out into the lake to allow the move. The day evolved into a dock-wide party when tension turned to relief as all the floating homes were reconnected to their moorings.

Heinz moved in in 2001 and has no regrets. He says:

'I love that I have no grass to mow, no leaky basement... Seriously though, it's not all that different from living in an apartment, with a fairly tight-knit community. I just love being on (or even near) the water; even the rain splashing down looks somehow more attractive here than on asphalt.'

Photography: Lagerquist & Morris

ABOVE: *Shingles clad the exterior and locally built Douglas Fir tilt-turn windows allow plenty of light and breeze to enter the home.*

RIGHT: *Moving day needed a lot of cooperation from all of Heinz's neighbours as their homes had to be moved to allow his in.*

ABOVE: *The basement features an underwater viewing porthole.*

LEFT: *Floor-to-ceiling windows allow lots of natural light to flood in and create a dramatic living space.*

ABOVE: *The stone floor features geo-thermal radiant in-floor heating.*

BELOW: *Exposed steel ceiling trusses and light bamboo wood floors maximise the feeling of space on the upstairs level.*

Sequoia

Finlay McDonell uses *Sequoia* as his home for several months of the year. She is moored at Lough Boderg on the river Shannon in Ireland. He chose to live afloat because he'd always enjoyed being on the water and playing around with boats so he saw it as a natural progression to own a floating home.

Sequoia is a purpose-built log cabin measuring 30ft (9m) by 30ft (9m). She is constructed from Finnish pine on a galvanised steel floating platform which has been engineered to carry the weight of the cabin while retaining a stable base for comfortable living. Electricity is supplied via a shore connection and provides power for cooking, heating and hot water. Water is supplied from a shore connection, but the design can also be entirely self-sufficient using a generator for power and a filtration system to draw water from the lake or river where it is moored.

All of the windows are double glazed and the wood is 4in (10cm) thick so it is very well insulated for cold winters.

Finlay loves being close to nature with the ability to move his home if he gets tired of the view. It's a reasonably easy task to tow *Sequoia* to the other side of the river just for a change of scenery. Finlay says:

'For me being on the water is all about enjoying the outdoor environment. Having a barbecue and socialising outside on a traditional vessel can be frustrating with its limited deck space. The logboat with its very stable 6ft (1.8m) wide deck facilitates plenty of space for making the most of the outdoors. Be it for a barbecue with friends, mooring boats alongside or going for a paddle in my kayak first thing in the morning. The logboat provides me with my perfect base for playing around on the river.'

Photography: Finlay McDonell

LEFT AND BELOW: *Sequoia's interior is simple, functional and requires very little maintenance.*

ABOVE: *Double-glazed windows fold out to allow good ventilation in summer.*

RIGHT: *The entrance features a small porch.*

ABOVE: *Wildlife at the door.*

RIGHT: *The deck allows plenty of space to moor other boats.*

Motor Cruisers and Motor Yachts

Anastasia III

Moored at Clear Lake, Texas, USA, *Anastasia III* is home to Keith Emmons. The vessel – a Krogen 42 – was built in Taiwan in 1986 and Keith has lived aboard for six years. She is 42ft (12.6m) long and the design is based on a traditional fishing trawler but is built in modern composite materials. Her forerunners were used for catching shrimp and spending many days out at sea, so her nautical pedigree is without question. However, it is unlikely the captains of such ships would have enjoyed the style and comfort that Keith enjoys in *Anastasia III*.

He has spent the last two years upgrading her navigation equipment so that he can spend more time doing what he loves – long-distance cruising. A full tank of fuel gives *Anastasia III* a cruising range of 2000 nautical miles or more.

Keith chose a life afloat aboard *Anastasia III* because of the freedom it gives him. He says:

'I love the freedom and atmosphere. This is real waterfront property! There are always lots of nice people around, or you can just be secluded if you like. No property taxes and if I don't like where I am I can start the engine and move.' The only downside for Keith is that he could do with more space; he is 6ft tall (1.8m) and is constantly banging his elbows in the shower.

Cooking and hot water are provided by bottled gas, with a stern mounted barbecue for outdoor cooking. The main engines also generate hot water when cruising, and a large battery bank and generator keep all the ship's systems running, including an air conditioner, when away from a shore connection.

ABOVE: *Anastasia III anchored.*

LEFT: *The stern showing barbecue and swimming platform.*

Photography: Keith Emmons

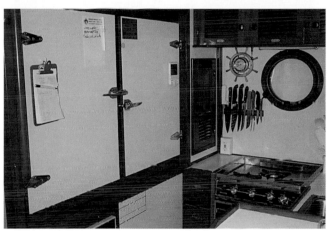

FAR LEFT: *The entrance to the bathroom from the bedroom.*

LEFT: *The master bedroom.*

BELOW LEFT: *The galley.*

BOTTOM LEFT: *The main living area.*

BOTTOM RIGHT: *The view from the deck during one of Keith's trips.*

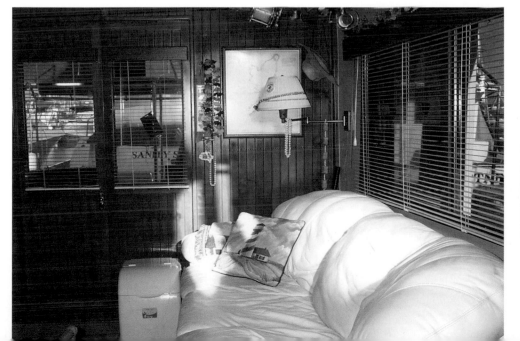

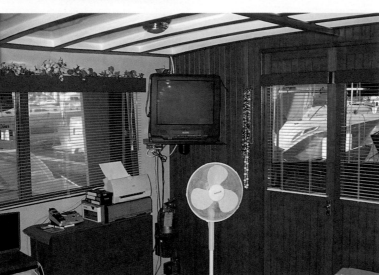

TOP LEFT AND RIGHT:
The galley aboard Anastasia III.

LEFT: *The main living area.*

ABOVE: *Happy times afloat.*

RIGHT: Anastasia
III *during a blessing of
the fleet.*

MIDDLE AND
RIGHT: *All lit up for a
boat parade at Keith's
home mooring.*

Narrowboats

Carpe Diem

Steve and Jennifer Davis live onboard *Carpe Diem*, a 60ft (18m) long narrowboat. Their home mooring is at Frampton-on-Severn on the Gloucester and Sharpness Canal.

They chose a life afloat for two reasons, the first was to enable them to live cheaply enough so that Steve could retire early, and secondly to provide a means of seeing some of the hidden bits of the British countryside. They have lived afloat since 2001.

For most of the year *Carpe Diem* is on the move. Steve and Jennifer's ambition is to cruise all the waterways in England and Wales that are safely navigable by narrowboat. They return to their home mooring in winter when repairs to the canal sometimes hinder progress.

Space is very important on a narrowboat so they opted to have all of their furniture built-in (as opposed to free-standing). Every bit of space under the furniture has been maximised, for example a section of the settee in the main living area doubles as a wine cellar. The living space and galley area have been kept as a single open room, with large windows and light wood to help give an illusion of space.

Carpe Diem has been designed for 'all-weather' cruising. She can be steered from the top step of the engine room with the stern doors closed and the hatch partly closed. There is a small heater (running off the engine cooling water) blowing hot air across the top step to keep your feet warm.

Cooking is by gas and heating is provided by a diesel boiler plus a diesel stove in the main living area. The boat has plenty of heating capacity. Steve and Jennifer have been iced in, with temperatures down to minus 8 degrees Centigrade, and remained warm and cosy inside.

ABOVE AND RIGHT: *Carpe Diem moored in Coventry basin next to a statue of James Brindley who built many of Britain's canals.*

Photography: Steve Davis

FAR LEFT: *The galley and the main living area.*

LEFT: *The forward deck with a cover to keep the weather out.*

ABOVE: *The stern cabin contains the engine and washing machine.*

RIGHT: *The settee with wine cellar underneath.*

BOTTOM FAR LEFT: *The master bed made up for sleeping…*

BOTTOM LEFT: *…and travelling.*

ABOVE: Enseabee *sits peacefully on her mooring.*

Enseabee

Nigel Burrows calls *Enseabee* home. She is an unusual vessel because she is built to enable her to travel the British narrow canals and so has maximum width dimensions of 7ft (2.1m) but she has been styled along the lines of a Dutch barge. A traditional narrowboat has an open steering position, but *Enseabee* has a fully enclosed wheelhouse which keeps the steerer warm and dry. It can also be lowered for very low bridges.

She is 56ft (16.8m) long and moored in Stone, Staffordshire. Nigel chose to live afloat because he loved the peace and quiet of the canals as well as the friendliness of other canal users. She is designed so that two people can cruise in comfort but with space for a few guests to join them when required.

Nigel completed the interior himself after having the shell built at a boatyard nearby. The fit-out involved over 2,000 hours of hard work but he enjoyed it immensely. Now he has more time on his hands, he and his partner Anne intend to get out cruising and explore more of the British canal system and later over to France.

It can be quite a challenge to squeeze all of the comforts of home into a space under 7ft (2.1m) wide, but Nigel has managed it with some flair. *Enseabee* has everything they need for travel and when moored.

Heating and cooking needs are satisfied by a diesel stove. It heats the water, runs radiators and a towel rail. There is no gas on the boat; *Enseabee* has a sophisticated electricity management system which supplies power for the lights, refrigeration, a small electric stove – which is a back-up to the diesel one – and the washing machine. A series of batteries and a 230v generator on the main engine provide all the power needed for life onboard.

Photography: Paul Cookson

LEFT: *The wheelhouse and steering position.*

ABOVE: *The dining area.*

BELOW: *The washing machine fits neatly under a cupboard containing the hot water tank and airing cupboard.*

BOTTOM: *The master bedroom.*

BOTTOM LEFT: *The galley.*

Iris №3

The design of *Iris №3* reflects the working tug narrowboats used on the canals in the UK around the turn of the 20th century but she was actually built in 1989. The long, low foredeck and small portholes with recessed panels are the details that distinguish it from a more traditional narrowboat.

Simon Sparrow calls *Iris №3* home at Willowtree Marina in west London. She is 53ft (16m) long and he has lived onboard since 2006.

Because of their width restrictions, making a home in a narrowboat can be a challenge. Simon's approach has been to make the interior open-plan with white painted walls, and thanks to a large skylight in the roof and lots of portholes, *Iris №3* feels light and spacious.

Simon has renovated and remodelled several areas of the interior, including using some wood he shipped over from his native New Zealand (Rimu), which he used to build a worktop and the fold-out table in the saloon.

Simon has done a lot of travelling in *Iris №3*, with his girlfriend, and this is one of the aspects that he loves about boat ownership. Some of the trips have been long ones but others have been a quick trip to the local pub.

The decision to buy a boat to liveaboard wasn't an easy one but it is one Simon doesn't regret.

'I thought if I didn't try it now, when would I? It's been a steep learning curve, but I'm very happy I took the risk and did it. Some of my friends don't understand, but most think it's great and enjoy dipping their toes into the boating world when they visit.

'I enjoy being close to water and seeing all the wildlife that lives in the marina, even in a city like London. I find being on the boat quite relaxing and peaceful and it makes a welcome refuge from my corporate life, which involves a lot of travel and meetings. Being able to go away on trips and take your home with you is still a fantastic novelty.'

ABOVE: *Iris №3 moored at Sonning on Thames during a trip upriver.*

RIGHT: *Simon reminds himself why it is called a narrowboat.*

FAR RIGHT: *A misty morning enjoyed aboard* Iris №3.

Photography: Simon Sparrow

FAR LEFT AND ABOVE: *Natural timber and white painted walls create a contemporary feel.*

LEFT: *The bathroom.*

 RIGHT AND FAR RIGHT: *The bed is under the low foredeck; the hatch steps are removed at night.*
BELOW: *A solid-fuel stove provides heat and Simon has even squeezed in a small office space.*

Journeyman

One sunny Saturday morning in 2005 Nick Alexander spotted a boat advertised on eBay. 24 hours later he made a bid which was accepted, three days later he was the proud owner of a 70ft (21m) long narrowboat called *Journeyman*.

'I would only have squandered the money on food and heating for my family otherwise,' said Nick.

This is Nick's first boat and two years have passed since his initial purchase. He found that since buying the boat – which he saw as a summer toy – he has spent more and more time on her each week, even through the winter. Now he only makes the occasional visit home to check he hasn't been forgotten.

Journeyman was built in 1985 as a one-off design for a professional carpenter who fitted out the interior himself. There is a traditional engine room that houses a vintage Lister JP3 engine. The engine, manufactured in 1929, had a previous life driving a fairground generator. It has since been fully restored and creates interest wherever it goes.

Journeyman's home mooring is currently at the Lazy Otter Marina, Stretham, Cambridgeshire and is well placed to explore several local places of interest by boat. Nick's travels so far have amounted to around 100 miles per year – on average one trip per fortnight.

Nick's initial enthusiasm on eBay has turned him from a boat novice to a full time liveaboard and he doesn't regret it for a minute.

'I wanted to have a compact, moveable, fun and cheap to run home – what I ended up with is a cramped; sometimes pretty firmly fixed thanks to lock closures; miserable (the combination of rain, rain, more rain, and leaks); and bank-breaking money pit. But would I swap it? Not on your sweet life!'

ABOVE AND FAR LEFT: *Journeyman on her home mooring at the Lazy Otter Marina.*

LEFT: *Detail of the tiller.*

Photography: Gary Cookson

LEFT: Journeyman on her home mooring — Nick loves the peace and quiet of living afloat.

BOTTOM LEFT: The main living area has a table and desk crafted from solid pieces of timber.

BOTTOM: The galley features lots of timber and a full size stove powered by bottled gas.

FAR LEFT: Journeyman's *galley with the bathroom beyond.*

LEFT: *A solid-fuel stove provides heat and has a back-boiler to heat radiators.*

BELOW: *The stern cabin with traditional detailing and engine controls.*

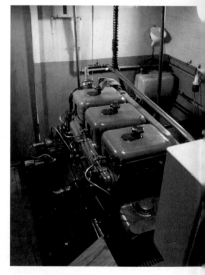

ABOVE: *A vintage Lister JP3 engine powers Journeyman and has a dedicated engine room.*

FAR LEFT: *The master bedroom.*

LEFT: *The bathroom.*

Tugs

Pelican

The *Pelican* is a former ocean-going tugboat, and at 100ft (30m) long and 27ft (8.1m) wide is one of the larger vessels in this book.

Pelican's occupants are Lorraine and Simon Bradley, their two dogs, Pugsley and George, two cats, Shankley and Paisley and a ferret called Ernie. They have been living aboard for seven years.

Pelican was built in 1967 and originally named *Dunosprey*. Based in Belfast, Northern Ireland, she was moved to London in 1992. In 1993 she was sold and renamed *Linda Bennett* and remained working on the Thames and Medway rivers until she suffered total engine failure in 1996.

Lorraine and Simon bought the tug in a neglected state in 1998 and began the process of converting her into a unique floating home. They stripped out the massive engine and associated machinery and converted the resulting space into a huge living area.

They retained as many of her original features as possible so that from the outside she still looks like a working tugboat. Inside, the mess room and crew quarters were incorporated into the conversion and are now used as a breakfast area and guest bedrooms respectively.

Pelican is moored at a dedicated marina for residential craft near Rochester, Kent. Lorraine and Simon chose to live afloat because they wanted a change. Lorraine says:

'We spent almost two years looking into the possibility before we took the plunge. We can now honestly say it was the best decision we have made and would only go back to land if we had no other choice.

'We love the community spirit, if you need help then there is always someone willing to give a hand, and if you want solitude then people respect that as well.'

ABOVE: Pelican *on her home mooring.*
LEFT: *The ship's mascot.*

LEFT: *Pelican has a large deck area for outdoor living. All of the original equipment used for towing has been left in place and restored.*

TOP: *The original ship's wheel.*

MIDDLE AND BOTTOM: *The original ship's telegraphs have been incorporated into the living area.*

TOP AND RIGHT: *The main living area, formerly the engine room.*

ABOVE: *The view from the gallery.*

TOP LEFT: *The galley adjoining the mess room.*

MIDDLE LEFT: *The original ship's mess room now adjoins the galley and is a great spot for breakfast.*

LEFT: *The wheelhouse with spectacular views.*

ABOVE: *The bathroom.*

TOP RIGHT: *The main living area has a large clear hatch to let lots of light in.*

TOP RIGHT: *The master bedroom.*

RIGHT: *One of the two guest bedrooms; both utilise the original crew's quarters with custom built double beds.*

ABOVE: *Quo Vadis is one of several classic ships moored in Gouda's harbour.*

Quo Vadis

Tugboat *Quo Vadis* is home to Marco Hoogendijk and Tamara Berends in Gouda, the Netherlands. She is moored in a harbour that caters specifically for historically important ships.

Quo Vadis is 69ft (21m) long and was built in 1940 in Ijsselmonde, the Netherlands, but during the Second World War, while she was still under construction, the German occupying forces claimed her and put her to work. In 1946 the vessel was returned to her original owner.

Unlike many ex-working vessels, *Quo Vadis* is in original condition and her layout is almost identical to how she was when first built. Marco and Tamara live on her in the same space her crew would have used. She is a fairly large ship, but because she is a tugboat built primarily for towing, the living area is relatively small – the largest space on the ship is taken up by the engine.

Marco and Tamara chose a life afloat as a natural progression from their love of water. Both of them grew up learning to sail around Gouda and were involved with the Sea Cadet Corps for many years. Neither plan ever to go back to a house.

Marco bought *Quo Vadis* in 2000 and moved onboard, Tamara joined him two years later. They have everything they need for comfortable living afloat including diesel-powered central heating, with radiators throughout the boat, gas cooking facilities, a washing machine, and the ability to occasionally tow large ships.

Marco and Tamara travel regularly in *Quo Vadis*, often in the company of other vessels from their harbour, and find it great fun to have neighbours who share their love of classic ships. They always enjoy going on holiday in their home because they don't have to pack.

Photography: Tamara Berends

TOP LEFT: *The main living area.*

ABOVE: *Stairs lead down to the crew quarters.*

LEFT: *Quo Vadis on her home mooring.*

TOP LEFT: *Marco and Tamara utilise the ship's original sleeping quarters.*

TOP: *The galley.*

ABOVE: *The wheelhouse.*

LEFT: *The entrance to the engine room.*

Yachts and Motorsailers

Sydney Sundancer

John and Lynne Boyce have an enviable lifestyle; they live aboard their luxurious sailing yacht *Sydney Sundancer* and divide their time between picturesque Sydney Harbour and the tropical paradise of the Whitsunday Islands on the Great Barrier Reef, Australia.

Sydney Sundancer is both their home and their business. They have combined their love of sailing, travel and great food and turned it into a thriving charter business – John is a master mariner and Lynne is a master chef.

Every year for the last 19 years they have sailed the 1,200nm north to the Whitsunday Islands from Sydney in June and returned in early November.

John and Lynne had *Sydney Sundancer* built in 1986 to their own custom design and incorporated several special features including a built-in ironing board. This was the subject of much discussion during construction, and has been used twice in nearly 20 years! She is is 54ft (16.2m) long and has sleeping accommodation for up to 12 people. John and Lynne prefer to host up to three couples in their own private cabins while they have their own quarters in the stern of the ship. The large rear deck has an area for alfresco dining and can be completely enclosed.

John and Lynne chose a life afloat to further their lifelong fascination with the sea and to spend more time doing what they love. John says:

'We get million dollar views without the high taxes! I love looking out of the portholes and seeing 18-footers flying past at water level with Sydney Opera House and Harbour Bridge in the background; standing on the bow of the yacht, watching dolphins swimming below; jumping off the transom to swim with magnificent fish and amazing corals. All this and earning a living from making guests happy while sharing their adventure in paradise.'

ABOVE: *The steering position and main entrance.*

LEFT: *View of the stern deck with dining area.*

FAR LEFT: *Sydney Sundancer at anchor during a trip to the Whitsundays.*

TOP: *The galley.*

RIGHT: *The ship's interior features beautiful teak detailing.*

ABOVE: *Looking towards the stern of the ship from the main entrance hatch.*

LEFT: *An en-suite guest bathroom.*

BELOW: *The crew's quarters.*

BOTTOM: *Bedroom number one.*

Trimilia

There can't be many homes that had a history of saving lives, but David and Moira Jay can make that claim about their ship *Trimilia*. She was formerly called *Prudential*, the lifeboat in service at Ramsgate between 1925 and 1953. She is credited with saving 330 lives in normal service and then during the Second World War she rescued 2800 troops during the Dunkirk evacuation in 1940. She is a registered historic vessel and official 'Dunkirk Little Ship'. After she retired in 1953, she was converted into a houseboat and then later into a ketch rigged sailing ship.

Trimilia is 48.6ft (14.8m) long and is now the permanent home of David and Moira, and their dog Tilly. Their home mooring is at Tidemill Yacht Harbour, Woodbridge, Suffolk. David also runs his business from the boat. They have lived aboard since 2005.

They chose to live afloat after buying a small motor sailing boat to use at weekends. They found themselves spending more time onboard than at their cottage so they decided to buy a bigger boat and move aboard full-time.

David and Moira described the positive aspects of their lifestyle:

- Being able to take your home elsewhere.
- Meeting new people around the marina – in particular visiting Dutch boats.
- Lying in bed enjoying the water reflections on our cabin wall and ceilings or listening to rain on the coach roof.
- Relaxing in the rear deck hammock, cold beer in hand, watching the coming and going of boats in the marina and on the river.
- Living a life that is simply different.

David and Moira have taken *Trimilia* on a few trips in the local area but have plans afoot to travel the waterways of Europe and further afield as soon as time permits.

ABOVE: *Trimilia on her home mooring in Woodbridge, Suffolk.*

LEFT: *A proud display of* Trimilia's *Dunkirk evacuation medals.*

Photography: David Jay

LEFT: *The entrance to the wheelhouse.*

BELOW LEFT: *Ship's compass.*

BELOW MIDDLE: *A plaque celebrating the 60th anniversary of the Dunkirk evacuation.*

BELOW: *Traditional ventilator in polished brass.*

ABOVE: *The main living area features a diesel-fired heater with a traditional look in-keeping with the interior.*

TOP LEFT: *Trimilia's well equipped galley was designed by David and hand-made by a retired shipwright and fellow lifeboat owner.*

FAR LEFT: *A corridor, with engineer's berth, leading to the engine room and guest sleeping quarters and office.*

LEFT: *The master bedroom with large built-in storage below.*

ABOVE: *Tilly keeps watch in the main living area.*

The Future?

What will floating homes of the future look like? Italian naval architect Giancarlo Zema has a vision, and these two vessels show the way a life afloat may evolve.

Trilobis 65 is a semi-submerged dwelling environment. It is 66ft (20m) long and designed for habitation by six people at sea. It is designed for living in bays, atolls and maritime parks in more tropical climates. The shape of *Trilobis 65* allows several units to moor together, creating island colonies.

The main aim of the project is to allow anyone to live in a unique environment through a self-sufficient, non-polluting dwelling cell. Light, heat and propulsion are all powered by electricity generated onboard via hydrogen fuel cells, solar panels (the external skin of the vessel would be covered in photovoltaic cells) and wind generators.

There are four separate levels connected by a spiral staircase. The top level is 11½ ft (3.5m) above sea level. The next level is at 4½ ft (1.4m) above sea level and hosts the daylight zone with all services and allowing outdoor access. The third level is situated at 2½ ft (0.8m) below sea level, semi-submerged, and is devoted to the night-time zone. Finally, at 10ft (3m) below sea level, totally submerged, there is the underwater observation bulb, an intimate and meditative place.

The second vessel, the *Jellyfish 45* (see page 126) is a similar structure but designed to be permanently moored. Its spacious dimensions are 11ft (3.3m) high with a diameter of over 16ft (4.8m).

Both vessels would be constructed in steel for the hull and aluminium for the superstructure. The submarine globes would be moulded acrylic with a high compressive resistance. Construction would use the same technology currently used on deep-sea and tourist observation submarines.

ABOVE: Trilobis 65 *underway.*
LEFT: Trilobis 65 — *the underwater observation and seating area.*

Images: *Giancarlo Zema Design Group*

TOP LEFT AND TOP:
Trilobis 65 — *the main living area with spiral stairs to the underwater observation and seating area.*

ABOVE AND LEFT:
Trilobis 65 — *the bedroom and below sea level seating.*

LEFT: *Jellyfish 45 moored.*

TOP AND ABOVE: Jellyfish 45 — the main living area with spiral stairs to the underwater observation and seating area.

ABOVE: Jellyfish 45 — the underwater observation and seating area.

LEFT: Jellyfish 45.

About the author

A writer, designer, publisher and keen renovator, Gary Cookson was introduced to boats at an early age thanks to growing up in a family of boat enthusiasts – though at the age of three he preferred to play with his toy cars in the bottom of his parents' racing dinghy rather than going sailing. His childhood disinterest soon turned into a love affair with all things nautical.

Gary turned to a liveaboard lifestyle after discovering a rusted and neglected Dutch sailing barge in the mud of the River Medway, Kent, UK.

After a two year gruelling refit including a few costly mishaps and a near sinking, his 72 ft (22m) barge was transformed into a comfortable floating home moored on the River Thames.

'A home afloat is definitely a fun way to live' says Gary. 'There's nothing better than watching the sunset from the deck of your own waterside residence and the satisfaction that comes from building and maintaining a unique home.'